The Gypsy
in
Northwest America

Gypsy Dance Group, Cracow, Poland.

The Gypsy
in
Northwest America

Gabrielle Tyrner-Stastny

The Washington State American Revolution Bicentennial Commission
1977

Contents

Illustrations

Foreword

The author brings a remarkable background to this study of Gypsy tradition. As an anthropologist, she trained at Heidelberg, in Germany; the Sorbonne, in France; and the Allahabad University, in India. A native of Austria, Dr. Tyrner-Stastny has traced the beginnings of Gypsy history back to India and Pakistan. Most Americans tend to associate the Gypsies with Europe, especially the Balkan countries, but the author shows that those nations, such as Rumania and Hungary, were only mid-passage in the Gypsy world migration. In every *gajo* (non-Gypsy) there may be some envy for the apparently free and unfettered existence of the *Romani* (Gypsies). Much of their vaunted freedom has always been due to their mobility. Someone said that a Gypsy is only comfortable "when his home is on wheels." But the author shows that, in the Pacific Northwest as well as in other regions, Gypsies are being absorbed into urban centers, surrendering the ancient freedom of constant travel. The problems of most ethnic groups in adaptation and assimilation are now theirs — but with some startling variations. The author elaborates on these variations in her careful study.

Gabrielle Tyrner-Stastny has worked with Gypsy communities in Seattle, Tacoma and Spokane and at present teaches ethnic history at the University of Washington, where she may draw upon personal experience with special projects involving the Gypsies. Her opening statement about the Gypsy campfires and music triggered a boyhood memory for me. I remember, in those long-ago days in western New York, the arrival of the Gypsy caravans with the coming of spring; the brightly painted, horse-drawn wagons, the colorful costumes, the dark skin and the flashing eyes.

Just south of Hornell, on the road to Canisteo, the Gypsy bands set up an encampment on what is still called "Gypsy Hill". Some evenings, the winds of April carried the smoke of their campfires and the sound of Gypsy music to the valley below. "Gypsy Hill" was off-limits to Hornell children — not because of Gypsy restrictions but because of the local folklore which hinted that errant boys might disappear forever if they wandered onto the forbidden camp grounds. Most Americans of my generation could tell a similar tale. For example, what do you know about the old recipe for "Gypsy goulash" which begins "first, steal a chicken!"

The author confirms the depths of *gajo* superstition which many Americans retain in their absolute ignorance of Gypsy history. She also sketches the darker passages of recent history, such as the plan by which Hitler and his Nazi henchmen set out to exterminate the Gypsy along with the Jew in Germany and the conquered nations of World War II. The Holocaust was a Gypsy, as well as a Jewish, nightmare.

No project in this ethnic history series has been more exciting or worthwhile to me than this contribution by Gabrielle Tyrner-Stastny. It is our hope that readers will be inspired to search for additional material, such as that listed in the bibliography, and that this fascinating book will persuade other historians to pursue the subject in depth. As with most of the ethnic histories in this series, the field for study and publication is nearly virgin territory.

Bruce Le Roy
Chairman
Washington State American
Revolution Bicentennial Commission

The Gypsy in Northwest America

Introduction

Almost everybody can conjure a picture of a Gypsy—particularly a Gypsy woman. She will have dark, flashing eyes, wear a full skirt, a coin necklace, hoop earrings and a bandana tied tightly around her head. Of course she will be telling fortunes; reading a palm or gazing into a crystal ball. The image has been used on television to sell a variety of products.

Older Americans can remember real women who looked like that, and men almost as colorful, with a bright scarf tied around their necks, going from house to house sharpening knives and repairing pots in the rural areas. They would also sell horses and fix roofs. Sometimes they would steal chickens, but more often, they were simply expected to do it, so the local police would usher them out of town at nightfall. Then, as darkness came, their fires would begin to flicker at the camping site, where the colorful painted caravans were clustered together. Sometimes the sound of singing would be heard, gay or melancholy songs in a language unlike any other spoken on the American continent.

Where have they disappeared, all these colorful Gypsies? Have they become as extinct as their horse-drawn caravans, which are now rented to adventurous tourists in some parts of Europe by an enterprising travel agency? Everyone remembers them as having countless children. What has happened to these, generation after generation? Have they all become middle class American businessmen and housewives? Where have all the Gypsies gone?

They are in our midst. Now mostly urban, they no longer wander about the countryside, plying their traditional trades. Many are settled and live in houses. They are no longer instantly recognizable; like other ethnic groups, they save their colorful costumes for ceremonial occasions. The men, particularly, may be mistaken for Chicanos, Italians, Greeks, East Indians or Native Americans. There are an estimated half million of them in the United States.

Yet "estimated" is perhaps too much to say. There is such a range of estimates, based on so little that could pass for statistics, that "intuitively guessed" might be a better term. These guesses, made by "experts", range from 20,000 to one and a half million. The lowest

1

estimate was made by a sociologist on the questionable grounds that "almost all the Gypsy adults I have met anywhere in North America know of nearly all the other families I have met."[1] The uppermost figure was estimated by the U.S. delegate of a new Paris-based Gypsy organization, who is probably the only Gypsy university professor in North America.[2]

In the year before the Bicentennial, a book appeared which referred to Gypsies as "the hidden Americans".[3] Many other writers have referred to them, particularly in present-day North America, as "invisible". They rarely identify themselves in the census, they change their names and residences frequently, they maintain their strong inner identification with their group while outwardly merging with their environment. A Canadian Gypsy writer, also unique in North America, where the majority of Gypsies are illiterate, says that in their invisibility lies their strength.

> It is not without good reason that many people consider them to be extinct, for (they) themselves do everything in their power to perpetuate the myth of their non-existence . . . they merge into the mass of strangers on the street . . . they change their names as often as they change their houses."[4]

The superficial adaptations, made again and again throughout their history, have enabled them to maintain the inner core of their culture to a degree that might be the envy of many more visible minorities now struggling to retrieve the remnants of their culture from the American melting pot. The clothing is no longer distinctive, particularly for the men; the horse-trader has become a used-car dealer, the wagon a mobile home or even a house. The ancient communication system of trail markings has been replaced by long-distance telephoning. Most families own a television set. And yet, it must seem, miraculously, the old ways continue to dominate their lives; the Gypsies are essentially unassimilated.

The mechanisms of maintaining invisibility have varied from time to time and place to place. They include changing names, and dates of birth, unannounced and unrecorded shifts of residence, and official identification with some other ethnic group. Ronald Lee, the Canadian Gypsy writer mentioned above, describes "the culture of invisibility" from first-hand experience:

> He is invisible and he has many weapons. You have a name but he has two: one you will never know and one he is always changing. Today he is Tom Jones, yesterday he was William Stanley, and tomorrow he might be Adam Strong.[5]

While the Gypsy name *(nav romano)* never changes, the name for the outside world *(nav gajikano)* is extremely variable, as Lee suggests. He gives the example of a well-traveled European coppersmith who, while in France, called himself Jean Malin, in Italy Giovaninni Malinni, in Spain Juan Malino, and in Canada Johnny Malone. His Gypsy name remained always O Vanya le Koliasko, or Vanya, the son of Kolia.[5]

When crossing borders, Vanya may have had a passport in any of these nationalities or none. Gypsies have never formally recognized national frontiers and find them, especially when they are still leading the nomadic life, a great nuisance. When essential, they will "acquire" passports; a group of Gypsies recently detained by immigration authorities in Quebec had in their possession a number of West German passports, the exact number of which were reported missing by the German consul.

The International Romani Committee, an organization trying to have Gypsies taken seriously as a nationality in Europe, has appealed to the U.N. and the Council of Europe to facilitate border crossings for the still-nomadic groups, whose kinship network and sources of livelihood are not confined to one country. The Gypsies have always lived as strangers within their host societies; their migration routes were not determined by national borders or international treaties. This was partly from choice—they see themselves everywhere as a separate people—and partly because of the universal hostility of the *gajo*, or non-gypsy.

The *gajo* for the Gypsy, like the *goy* for the orthodox Jew, is the outsider who is at once powerful and despicable. From him comes both persecution and ritual defilement. Contact with him is a threat to the individual and to the culture, yet essential for survival. He is to be feared, outwitted, but not emulated.

The Gypsies' strong desire to escape notice of *gajo* officials (fear of persecution) and at the same time keep the *gajo* socially at arm's length (fear of defilement) has led to the "culture of invisibility". If questioned, they tell the *gajo* what he wants to hear or whatever would provide the best cover. If possible, they will deny being Gypsies at all, as they know that in most places a special set of rules exists for them. As with orthodox Jews, this fear and strong desire for separateness is built into their culture. Even very young children have learned techniques for avoiding and misleading the *gajo*, escaping the detection of officials and curiosity-seekers.

This attitude has compounded the difficulty of gathering any

3

accurate information, historical or statistical, about the Gypsies as a minority group in America. The fact that the overwhelming majority are illiterate—they see schools as the greatest *gajo* threat to their culture—has prevented the formation of a group of "middle men" who could act as cultural intermediaries. There are, of course, the legendary "kings" who shuttle back and forth between *gajo* officials and the community procuring welfare, controlling licenses, etc., but they are only playing a traditional and very limited role as economic inter-mediaries. Their "kingship" is a convenient myth perpetuated for the *gajo*, who likes to believe he is dealing with authority figures. They are, in fact, strangers in the *gajo* world like other members of their community, and can interpret its values only in terms of their own.

The Gypsies have suffered harrassment and persecution in various degrees of severity from every society in which they have found them-selves in the course of their wanderings. Stereotypes of Gypsies as thieves, vagrants and kidnappers abound throughout the world. Most Europeans can remember parents or nursemaids threatening them with "the Gypsies will come for you if you don't behave." One educated middle-aged Austrian now living in New York recalled how the Gypsies had almost "stolen" her as a small child.

> "I was playing outside the house where we stayed during summer vacations. The Gypsies were camped in a field nearby. An old Gypsy woman came and asked me if I would like to come with her to her wagon. I was ready to go, but my mother was chopping food in the kitchen and saw it outside the window. She came running out with the knife in her hand . . ."

When asked how she knew that the old woman had intended to kidnap her she replied, "Oh, they were always looking for children, they liked blond ones particularly."

In addition to property theft and kidnapping, Gypsies have been accused of witchcraft and even cannibalism in Europe. Pejorative associations about them have been built into the very language of the people around them, e.g., to "gyp" someone.

It is no wonder that the small but growing number of ethnically aware Gypsies resent such associations, unconscious as they may be on the part of the speaker. Most minority group members can attest to the effect that such casually used colloquial expressions have had on them: "he's an Indian giver", "I'll jew him down", "he doesn't have a Chinaman's chance", "keep your cotton-picking fingers out of there" etc.

In the English-speaking countries, many "Gypsies" have rejected

4

this *gajo* designation completely, not only because of its negative associations in the minds of the majority, but because it was derived from a mistaken notion of their origins as "Egyptians". They prefer to be called *Rom* ("man") or, because of the association of Rom with a particular group of Gypsies, *Romani,* a more inclusive term. However, only a few North American Romani have such an awareness. The majority continue to refer to themselves as Gypsies. Therefore, we will be using these terms interchangeably, after some clarification.

Definition of Rom

While the word Rom or Romani has recently been used as a generic term to replace "Gypsy", strickly speaking the Rom are a particular group of Gypsies—in the U.S., the overwhelming majority. They are speakers of *Romanes,* a highly inflected Indic language, and they were traditionally nomadic. They form a distinct ethnic group with four principal subdivisions, sometimes called tribes or "nations" *(natsia)*: the Kalderash or coppersmiths, who constitute the majority of American Rom; the Machwaya or traders, whose name is derived from an area in Yugoslavia where they once lived; the Lowara, mostly horse traders, a small group in the U.S.; and finally, the feared Churara, sometimes called "outlaw" Gypsies, sparsely represented in the U.S.

There are a number of non-Rom Gypsies (or Romanies, if they come to accept that term) whom many Washington State Rom refer to collectively as *Boyash.* These actually are sedentary Gypsies from Hungary and Rumania. There are also English Gypsies *(Romanichal),* Spanish Gypsies known as *Gitanos* in Spanish and *Gitanes* in French *(Kalé* in their own language, somewhat different from Romanes). There are also the *Manush* (the Sanskrit term for "Man") and *Sinti* (presumably derived from the province of Sind, now in Pakistan, which in turn was taken from the Persian designation for the Indus River) who are sedentary Gypsies found in France and Germany respectively.

None of these non-Rom groups are of much importance for this study of the Washington *Roma* (plural of Rom), who know of their existence and may have run into a few, but have little regular interaction with them. The Rom's general feeling is that Boyash and others are not "true Gypsies." Therefore, we will be dealing here exclusively with the Rom, although the term "Gypsy", when used in a historical or worldwide context, may have broader connotations.

5

A Backward Glance

After determining who the Rom are, we are confronted with the puzzling question of "where did they come from?" There had been theories of their origins ranging from Egypt to Chaldea. One of their own myths placed them in the Biblical area of Palestine at the time of Christ, where a Gypsy blacksmith was said to have been asked to forge the nails for the Crucifixion. A number of European historians, up to the 19th century, attempted to identify them with the Jews, another pariah people with a world-wide diaspora. In his early 19th century *Dictionnaire Infernal*, Collin de Plancy described Gypsies as "a race of Jews who had later become mixed with Christian vagabonds" after escaping to the forests of Europe when the Jews were appointed as scapegoats for the black plague that ravaged the continent in the middle of the 14th century.[7]

Interesting as all these theories were, there was no solid evidence for any of them. While the colorful caravans and fortune tellers had become a familiar sight for many centuries, it was not until the development of the science of comparative philology in the late 18th and early 19th centuries that the riddle of the Gypsies' origins was solved at last.

It was a Hungarian theology student at Leyden in the Netherlands who first noticed the uncanny resemblance between the language of the Hungarian Gypsies that he had so often heard in his homeland, and the language of some Indian fellow students. He enlisted the help of these students and together they compiled a vocabulary of about a thousand words, together with their meanings. When he returned to his home, he read this list of words to the Gypsies of his native district of Komora. They easily identified the meaning of almost all of them. Without a doubt, their language was closely related to the languages of North India. With this clue, a series of linguistic and ethnological studies in the 19th century determined beyond a reasonable doubt that the people miscalled "Egyptians" (from which "gypsy" is derived) originally came from India. Why they left when they did remains a mystery, though there has been much scholarly speculation, mainly linking the exodus to the Muslim invasions of India beginning in the 12th century. But there is no firm evidence for this. Linguists have also been able to trace the course of the Gypsies' travels and the duration of their stay in various countries through the loan words which they picked up along the way.

The linguistic evidence confirms what any observer familiar with Indian culture can observe: that despite centuries of superficial accul-

Gypsy Dance Group, Cracow, Poland.

turation to many different societies, despite a thousand years' absence and a complete lack of contact during that period, the essential customs, beliefs and institutions of Rom society are strikingly similar to those of Hindu India. The betrothal and marriage customs, the overriding concern with ritual purity and pollution, the *kris romani* or court of elders—all these and others have their counterparts in traditional Indian society. And this brings us to the greatest mystery of all: how can a culture and language with a rich oral tradition and countless mechanisms for self-preservation in the fact of outside pressures of all sorts have obliterated all consciousness of its origins?

In very recent years, there have been attempts to renew the links severed so long ago from both the Romani and Indian sides. In 1962 a book was published by the Indian Ministry of Information and Broadcasting entitled *Gypsies, Forgotten Children of India,* in which the author, Chaman Lal, attempts to ascertain that the gypsies regard India as their "Motherland". In 1973 an Indian Institute of Romani Studies was inaugurated at Chandigarh, capital of the Punjab, the area from which the Gypsies are believed to have originated. An international Romani Congress was held there in 1975, with delegates from many parts of the world. Much of this was in response to a series of international Romani organizations that sprang up in Europe in the 1960s, some of which adopted a return to the homeland—Romaestan, a Romani Israel presumably located, physically or spiritually, in India. These organizations, centered in Paris, were composed primarily of educated Rom or part-Rom in search of their roots. So far, they have had little influence in North America, despite the efforts of the Canadian delegate of the Comité International Rom, Ronald Lee, and the U.S. delegate, Ian Hancock.

Many Gypsy informants were incredulous when told that their people had originated in India. For them, Europe was their place of origin. Some identified India with American Indians and expressed sentiments similar to those of white ethnic majorities anxious to separate themselves from the non-white minorities. Even the old story of Egyptian origins is given little credence. One informant put it this way:

> "Our origins are supposed to be from India but we as Gypsies want to be identified from the European countries, from Yugoslavia, Czechoslovakia, Hungary. We are proud that people recognize us from that part of the world. People say you are Indians or East Indians or Pakastanians.
>
> I will not recognize that I am of Indian descent because I have no language, no food, no music, I don't have anything in common with India."

Another man said: "You try and tell my wife she's Indian, it's like telling her she's black." His wife agreed, and added, "I ain't Indian, my father's Greek, he was born in Athens."

Nevertheless, a few leaders have begun to show interest in the Gypsies' Indian legacy and questioned the author at length about comparions between Hindu and Romanes languages, between Indian and Rom culture. After the author's return from India, they requested to be shown her slides and films. As the film was being projected, they frequently asked me to hold a frame so they could get a better look at a particular gesture or item of clothing. "Look at the face on that woman," one would cry out, "she looks like my aunt." Another exclaimed when the film showed some Indian peasant women, small children astride their hips: "Look, they carry their kids like we do!"

When the Roma left India, presumably in several waves, they travelled through the Middle East and on to southeastern Europe, where we find the earliest records indicating that their presence on that continent came from Crete, Corfu and Greece in the early 14th century. The Greeks called them by the name of a heretical sect, *Atsigani*, from which derives the name by which Gypsies are designated in most European languages (e.g. German, "Zigeuner", Hungarian "Cigany", Spanish "gitano", etc.)

After a relatively long sojourn in Greece—judging by the amount of Greek vocabulary in Romanes—they moved on to Hungary and the Balkans, perhaps on the heels of the Turkish invasion. In some of these areas they became associated with the invaders, and in the 16th century German and Czech areas legislation was enacted expelling them as Turkish spies.

Gypsies appeared near the North Sea in 1417 carrying a safe-conduct letter from the Pope and calling themselves "Lords of Little Egypt". They asserted that they were condemned by God to wander for seven years to atone for the sin of their ancestors who had refused sanctuary to the Holy Family. This pious story had deeply impressed not only the Pope but the Emperor Sigismund of Hungary who gave them a letter to aid them on their voyage of penitence. It was clear that from their first appearance in Europe, the Rom had sized up the *gajo* shrewdly and manipulated them with great psychological skill in order to insure their own survival.

By the middle of the 15th century, Gypsies had spread throughout all of Europe, and the curiosity and tolerance with which they were initially treated had changed to hostility and discrimination. They were accused of witchcraft, thievery and kidnapping. Both Church and State passed laws against them. They soon found themselves perma-

9

Gypsy Dance Group, Cracow, Poland.

nently on the fringe of the societies in which they lived. In the succeeding centuries they were persecuted, killed, enslaved and offered incentives to assimilate. None of these attempts at "solving the gypsy problem" succeeded. They continued to survive, multiply and wander. In the late 19th century, they began to travel even farther, crossing not only mountains and frontiers but oceans as well.

They came to the New World with the large waves of immigration, scattering at first into rural areas in an attempt to continue their familiar life-style of the European countryside. They wandered about in caravans, going to carnivals, telling fortunes, observing Gypsy rules of territoriality and kinship.

This period lasted until about 1925 when, with increasing urbanization, nomadism began to decrease. Fewer winter camps were established first, then fewer summer camps as well. Cars had begun to take the place of horses, there was less unclaimed land on which to camp, and the Depression sharply curtailed the money that could be spent by Americans on "luxury" items like fortune-telling. After the election of Franklin D. Roosevelt and the inauguration of the New Deal, Gypsies began to flock to the large cities where they could avail themselves of welfare and relief programs. This entailed considerable cultural readaptation. During World War II, the process of change continued. As the wartime economy boomed, some gypsies for the first time undertook wage labor for the *gajo*. Because of gasoline rationing, their travelling was still further curtailed. The draft had to be evaded. It was a critical time in their history and contemporary observers predicted accelerating assimilation.[8]

But, as in the past, predictions about the Gypsies' demise were premature. Resources, technology, clothing, even living patterns changed and the Rom readapted, but the core of their culture remained intact, as always. And this they jealously preserved from contamination by the outside world.

Rom Society and Culture

What is this cultural core, so carefully guarded by the Rom through all their superficial changes? It could be summed up in one word *romania*. The *romania* is the moral order, the unwritten law and traditions by which the Rom live. It is through this order that strict boundaries are maintained between the Roma and the *gajo* world. Those who violate *romania* may be cast out from the community, temporarily or permanently. This is a strong sanction for enforcing conformity to the essentials of Rom culture.

11

Gypsy Musicians from Cracow, Poland.

The Kris Romani

The formal mechanism for imposing sanctions is the institution of the *kris romani* or Gypsy court. If a member of the community has seriously violated some aspect of the *romania*, the court may declare the individual *marimé* or polluted. This means avoidance by other members of the community. For the period of the sentence, even members of the person's own family are forbidden to share food with him. The importance of commensality as a symbol of social solidarity and the custom of "outcasting" suggest parallels to Indian culture.

The court meets for other matters, too, most commonly to settle marriage disputes which involve a return of a brideprice to a father-in-law, or to deal with the problem of elopement. The judges of the *kris* are elders who may be drawn from several lineages or *vitsi* (sing.: *vitsa*). In really big cases, they may come from different parts of the country. "Laws" may be changed by these courts, in which case the judges become legislators. In recent times a *kris* convened in Los Angeles to discuss new rules for dealing with elopement, settlement of "brideprice" and informing to *gajo* authorities (one of the various ways in which outsiders have traditionally been used to maintain the cohesion of Gypsy culture and society). The heads of *vitsi* from all over the country attended this *kris*.

Purity and Pollution

Concepts and practices related to purity and pollution affect every facet of the Rom's life. They determine where he lives, at what he works and how he relates to his family. A house formerly occupied by *gaje* is considered *marimé* (polluted) until appropriately purified. Certain occupations such as medicine and plumbing are considered *marimé* because those who practice them must come in contact with what is considered most defiling of all: excrements and female genitalia. There are among the Rom—as among Hindus—ritual taboos connected with menstruation, childbirth and sexual relations.

There are some acts or contacts which will make a Rom automatically *marimé*, without court sentence. The most dramatic instance of this is "skirt tossing", a powerful weapon in the hands of women. By tossing her traditionally ample skirts toward a man's head, raising them above her genitals or bringing his head in contact with her lower undergarments, a Romni (Rom woman) could break up fights, protect herself against violence and achieve revenge. It is enough for her to simply report such an act. The man will generally be considered *marimé* until she retracts her statement or he brings evidence before the *kris* that her statement was false. Thus women, although occupying a subordinate place in Rom society, have considerable power through their ability to pollute.

Thus, the concept of *marimé* is at once a powerful means of social control and a way of drawing strict boundaries between male and female, between upper and lower parts of the body, between Rom and *Gajo*. By performing an act considered *marimé*, the individual becomes subject to both sacred and secular retribution. He knows himself unclean and he may be formally outcast from the community.

Purity-pollution ideas and practices have been especially effective in maintaining boundaries between the Rom and the outside world, thus preserving their ethnicity even as they were adapting to new societies. Since the *gajo* is *marimé* by definition, great care must be exercised in relation to any social intercourse with him. Legitimately relations with *gaje* were essentially economic transactions. Although a *gajo* in a good working relation with a member of the community may be invited to a Rom home or feast *(slava)*, special eating utensils are generally reserved for such visitors.

Similar observances will be found in Hindu India. Casteless foreign visitors to an orthodox Brahmin home—particularly in rural areas—are given special dishes not used by other members of the family. Ritual pollution may be a cause for outcasting. It seems probable that the Rom customs related to purity and pollution represent a major portion of the Rom's no longer conscious Indian legacy.

It has also been suggested by a variety of observers that these customs derive from the Gypsies' nomadic past when extreme cleanliness—there are strict rules about the separation of bathing, drinking and laundry vessels—modesty and sexual taboos were essential for physical survival in the close-quartered life of the road.

Social Structure

The basic social unit in the nomadic as in the sedentary life is the extended family, which usually includes a couple, their unmarried children and their married sons and families. (This also conforms closely to the dominant Indian pattern, as does the continuing practice of arranged marriages at an early age.) Girls are considered an economic asset in terms of their earning capacity as fortune tellers; therefore the prospective groom's father may pay a considerable "brideprice", which often becomes a subject of dispute if the marriage breaks up. The relationship between the parents-in-law is important and there is a special name for it in Romanes, *xanamik*. Sutherland reports that in California there is an increasing tendency for the *xanamik* to be first cousins. This is believed to decrease the chances of friction between the two families and in Rom society (like Indian society) marriage is primarily a contract between families rather than individuals.[9]

The next social unit, after the family, is the *kumpania*. This is also the economic unit, which, whether it is traveling or stationary, controls the resources of a particular area.[10] These resources may include fortune-telling licenses, used-car dealerships, welfare, etc. No newcomer Rom can share in them without permission of the *kumpania* in the area, often expressed through a leader or *baro* ("big man"), the closest analogy in real Gypsy society to the legendary "Gypsy Kings".

A *baro* may extend his (or her) leadership beyond the *kumpania* to a whole *vitsa*, which may be scattered throughout a large area, but that is generally the outer limits of his power.[11] As a respected elder, he will probably also serve as a judge in the *kris romani*.

Rom and Gajo

The relationship between the Rom and their host societies has always been problematical. As we have seen, the curiosity and tolerance with which they were regarded when they first made their appearance in Europe with impressive safe-conduct letters from Church and State, gradually changed to suspicion and hostility. Like the Jews, with whom they were sometimes identified, they became pariahs everywhere in Europe, harassed by both religious and secular authorities. Unlike the Jews, they had no compunctions about adopting the religion—at least nominally—of the area in which they found themselves. But the churches often regarded their conversion with skepticism and treated them more like heathens than Christians. In 1560 an Archbishop of Sweden decreed that priests should refrain from christening and burying Gypsies.[12]

There were similar doubts about the sincerity of the conversions expressed in Muslim and Greek Orthodox ecclesiastical circles and numerous restrictions were placed on Gypsy converts. An Islamic divine warned his congregation not to give alms to Gypsies or the curse which they carried might transfer itself to them. In 19th century Bulgaria, Orthodox clergy declared that giving anything to Gypsies was a greater sin than theft.[13]

Secular authorities were even harsher. The rulers of European countries through which the Gypsies roamed tried everything from expelling them to enslaving them; from executing them to attempting to forcibly assimilate them. In the 18th century the Empress Maria Therese of Austro-Hungary made a major attempt to settle them in her domain. They were given housing, forbidden to travel or speak their language and, in many cases, their children were taken away from them to be raised by non-Gypsies. They were euphemistically called "New Hungarians."

And yet there was always a high degree of ambivalence in European attitudes toward the Gypsies, and much of this followed them to the New World. At the same time that they were being persecuted, they were romanticized. Their apparently free life-style, their refusal to be confined by the routines of sedentary people, made them envied at the same time that they were despised. Many American children who never had and perhaps never would see a Gypsy learned these lines of verse at an early age:

> The gypsies passed her little gate
> She stopped her wheel to see
> The brown-faced pair who walked the road
> Free as the wind is free
> And suddenly her little room
> A prison seemed to be . . .

The great 19th century French writer, Gustave Flaubert, attempted to analyze the hostility that he saw directed toward a small group of Gypsies by the settled citizens of Rouen. He wrote to Georges Sand:

"This hatred partakes of something very profound and very complex. One finds it in all orderly people. It is the hatred that one has for the bedouin, for the heretic, for the philospher, for the solitary being, for the poet; and in this hatred, there is fear."[14]

To Flaubert, by contrast, as to so many other European artists struggling to find themselves within the confines of bourgeois society, the Gypsies represented freedom. He found them "inoffensive as sheep".[15] Both these attitudes, of course, derive from an ignorance of Rom society—an ignorance which the Gypsies, in their long struggle to survive, did much to encourage.

The most horrifying expression of this ambivalence in modern times can be found in the prison memoirs of Rudolph Höss, commander of the Nazi extermination camp, Auschwitz, where thousands of Gypsies and others perished. The Gypsies, like the Jews of the world, had been singled out by Hitler for total annihilation, the final terrible parallel of their historic destinies in Europe.

16

Höss called the Gypsies his "best-loved prisoners" who delighted to play "even at work, which they never took quite seriously". It was not easy, he lamented, to drive them into the gas chambers as "they were by their nature as trusting as children".[16] Höss took pride in the playground built in the "Gypsy camp" of Auschwitz, where children could "run about to their heart's content and play with toys of every description" en route to their extermination.[17] He recalled how the SS officers loved to watch the Gypsies sing and dance. One officer organized an orchestra to give a concert at the camp. This event was interrupted, however, by a curfew during which fellow officers sent hundreds of Gypsies to the gas chambers.[18]

Educated European Gypsies are as aware of this terrible legacy as are Jews the world over. Monuments have been raised by them on the site of East European death camps. Reparations have been demanded from the German government by the World Romany Congress. Ronald Lee, the Canadian Gypsy who lived in England for many years, sings melancholy songs of the concentration camps. A distant relative of his, Clifford Lee, who made a journey retracing the footsteps of his people with a National Geographic writer and photographer, visited Dachau en route East. He came from the museum in which the horrors are documented to the last detail. Standing under the poplars planted by prisoners long since perished, he called down a Romanes curse on those who created Dachau.

In Auschwitz there was the special gypsy camp. You can find it on a map at the entrance behind the motto "Arbeit Macht Frei". (Work liberates). The notorious Dr. Mengele set up his medical experiments here. The order was given by Himmler to liquidate the Gypsy camp in April of 1944, when its usefulness to the Nazis had been exhausted. Out of some 20,000 Gypsies in this camp, only a few hundred survived. About 4,500 were killed in a single night of terror. They were called out of their barracks, given a special ration of bread and salami and loaded on trucks with the assurance that they were to be sent to a work camp. To further allay panic, the trucks drove in an opposite direction until darkness fell, then they circled and drove straight to the gas chambers and crematoria.[19]

A witness at the Auschwitz trial in Germany in 1964 testified:

> "Terrible scenes took place. Women and children were on their knees in front of Mengele and Boger crying 'Take pity, take pity on us'. Nothing helped. They were beaten down brutally, trampled on and pushed on to the trucks . . . Until far in the night I heard their cries and knew they were resisting. The Gypsies screamed all night . . . they sold their lives dearly."[20]

17

In the morning there were no more Gypsies in the camp.

Sometimes one will still come across them, European Gypsies, like European Jews, with a blue number tatooed on their forearms. The National Geographic editor, Bart MacDowell, encountered it in Germany, on the arm of Kitta Reinhardt, wife of the celebrated Gypsy musician Schuckenack* Reinhardt. She had been tattooed as a child in Auschwitz.[21] Ron Lee recalls a Hungarian Gypsy wedding in Toronto when, after much drinking, an old woman began to sing:

Oy marde ma, Mamo, hay shude ma ando baro shantso le mulensa . . .

"Oh they beat me Mother, and they threw me in the ditch with the dead,
They were all bleeding and I was covered with their blood,
Not my blood, Mother, but the blood of the dead Gypsies,
They threw them on top of me, Mother, the dead Gypsies,
The Germans killed them, Mother, and threw them in the ditch,
But I didn't die Mother, I didn't die,
I lived to be alone in the world, alone among the Gypsies."[22]

To this day, the word "Hitlari" is a vile epithet among German Gypsies, McDowell reports.[23]

But American Gypsies who have lost contact with Europe scarcely know about this episode in their history. Many of them have heard that Gypsies were killed in Europe, but they are not sure when and by whom. Their lack of historicity is very much in tune with their ideology of living for today, surviving another year in all its uniqueness. Like their Indian ancestors, they are traditionalists without a sense of history. Individual Gypsies who have survived the Nazi death camps, of course, will never forget. They are like the old emaciated woman described by McDowell who had lost husband and children to the gas chambers, sitting alone at the edge of the firelight in the German countryside. But for the Gypsies as a whole, world history means little. In this, they are profoundly different from the Jews, and for whom the Nazi holocaust has become a consuming collective memory, a historical nightmare from which there is no awakening.

While ambivalent attitudes towards the Gypsies continued in America as well as in Europe, persecution was sporadic and generally took the form of local police harrassment—escorting the Gypsies out of town at nightfall, keeping a close watch on their activities, arresting them for vagrancy or fortune telling, etc. The larger policy, if any

---

*A name derived from "Shukar nak" or "beautiful nose" in Romanes.

existed, was of a not-so-benign neglect. Few officials, outside of police and welfare authorities, concerned themselves with the existence of Gypsies as individuals and as an ethnic group. This attitude permitted the Rom to remain largely invisible until they were ready to make their appearance on the stage of American history.

The Rom of Washington State

The history of immigration in Washington contains no chapter on the Rom. But we know that by the turn of the century they had become very much a part of the scene at carnivals, in mining camps, on the outskirts of small towns. One 60-year-old Rom recalled hearing about Gypsies in Seattle when he was a small child traveling around with his family in the East.

An elderly resident of Roslyn, Washington, once a booming coal-mining town, remembered seeing the Gypsies every summer. "They used to rent store fronts on Pennsylvania Avenue (the main street!) and tell fortunes." His mother used to go down and "just talk to them" because, like herself, they came from Serbia and spoke her language.

In fact, Gypsies often made their headquarters in the immigrant quarters of a city or in a mining camp such as Roslyn, where a majority of the population was of immigrant origin. For these people, mostly of peasant stock, Gypsies were a familiar sight; but the transplants had brought with them from Europe all the familiar prejudices. "You had to watch them all the time," an elderly shopkeeper recalled, "or they'd steal you blind."

Another elderly man recalled how the police would run the Gypsies out of town at sunset. Naturally, he added, whenever anything was missing, they would get blamed. Sometimes they stole chickens but, he added, "they did it to eat" as compared with more recent outsiders, "who do it for fun."

The same man recalled another side of the *gajo* stereotype:

"A lot of the men would go have their fortunes told, but I don't know that it was for the fortunes. Those women used to dress something colorful, they'd wear flimsy transparent blouses . . ."

The rough miners of Roslyn, like *gaje* the world over, discovered that with the Gypsies, things are not what they seem. The come-on that lured them into the tent was followed by nothing more than a fortune. Any other notions were quickly discouraged by the sudden appearance of a male Gypsy.

The myth of Gypsy female promiscuity is a widespread one and, as all those who have come to know Rom culture can attest, one of the most factually unfounded of all stereotypes. There is scarcely any American ethnic group in which are found stricter controls of female sexuality. Marriages are arranged by parents at the time of puberty or shortly thereafter, sexual activity outside of marriage is strictly taboo and prostitution within the Gypsy culture is practically unheard of, though many Gypsy women have been arrested for "soliciting" outside their illegal or quasi-legal fortune-telling establishments. By *gajo* standards they may often be dressed provocatively (there is no taboo on exposure of the breasts as there is on that of the legs, so many Gypsy women favor low-cut blouses); moreover, they may use deceptively sexual lures to bring people into their *ofisia* or fortune-telling store front. The non-Gypsy male who assumes that this is a prelude to sexual relations is brusquely disabused of the notion at his first attempt, either by the woman herself or male relatives, who are never far away. The client may be bodily thrown out and threatened with a charge of attempted rape.*

There are economic reinforcements for the Roms' strict sexual morality for women. The institution of the brideprice requires, among other desirable qualities, chastity at the time of marriage for a girl. If a married woman leaves her husband or behaves in a manner disapproved by the community, her father-in-law can demand a refund.

There were some twenty-four nationalities in Roslyn and, one old-timer recalls, the Gypsies could speak to each of them in their own language. The little boys of 60 years ago used to go and watch the nomads at their camp outside of town. They camped in tents and caravans. The women wore full, brightly colored skirts and the married ones had the familiar scarf on their heads, a tradition still strictly adhered to today. They were covered with jewelry, preferably made from gold coins.

In some areas of the West, they might travel the routes of the migrant workers, who seasonally picked fruits, telling fortunes and plying their trades as they went. Often they were barkers or performers

---

*A sociologist in Vancouver, B.C., relates that he has examined police records of complaints made against Gypsy fortune tellers over a period of several years. Among the recurring themes he found was aggressive resistance on the part of Gypsy women to real or alleged sexual advances. He concludes that there wasn't anything in all the records which could accuse any Gypsy woman of practicing prostitution, nor had he ever come across any first-hand charges of that in North America. (Werner Cohn, *"The Persistence of a Relatively Stable Pariah Group: Some Reflections about Gypsies",* unpublished manuscript, n.d.)

at carnivals and, of course, there were the perennial fortune-telling tents.

Their caravans then, as their houses today, were filled with symbols of the occult and religious icons. Nevertheless, their attitude to religion and the supernatural remains casual. No Gypsy woman would dream of telling another Gypsy's fortune. That is a traditional art that has always been reserved for the *gajo*. As for the church, although baptism and funerals are conducted there, little of importance in life between those two events takes place in church. Saints' days are celebrated in Gypsy fashion with lavish feasts. Their special patrons are St. George and St. Anne. Some West Coast Gypsies have made the annual August pilgrimage to Quebec to celebrate the feast of St. Anne de Beauprès, at which Gypsies from all parts of North America congregate. It is the American counterpart of the pilgrimage to St. Maries-de-la-Mer in Southern France which, every May, draws Gypsies (and tourists) from all parts of Europe to pay homage to two Marys and their presumably Gypsy servant-companion, Sara le Kala ("the black"), who has never been canonized by the Church, but is the patron saint of millions of Gypsies.

The Population

A unique demographic survey conducted in the state of Washington in 1973 by a *gaji* (feminine form of *gajo*) anthropologist and a Tacoma Gypsy leader estimated there were between 800 and 1000 Rom in the state. [25] The main population concentrations are in Seattle, Tacoma and Spokane. Almost all the adult males are involved with used car dealing and many of the women are fortune tellers—despite the illegality of this activity in the state. A high percentage of families are on welfare.

Most of Washington's Rom are sedentary, living in houses or store-fronts for most of the year. In summer, there is a considerable amount of travel, making for population fluctuations. In addition, a serious conflict had developed, while the census was under way, between the Rom of Portland and another ethnic minority. Several Gypsy houses were robbed and burned. As a result, the whole community felt threatened and many sought sanctuary in Washington State, swelling the population figures.

Despite the difficulties inherent in counting any nomadic or semi-nomadic population, one can assume that the presence and support of a respected Rom leader, Miller Stevens, has made this survey more accurate than any previous estimates. Most *gajo* efforts at Gypsy census taking have been notoriously unsuccessful. Several individuals in the same family may use the same identical *nav gajikano* (*gajo* name) and the numbers, sex and residence of any household will be extremely variable. The presence of Miller Stevens, with his prestige and personal knowledge of the life situations of most of the informants, greatly reduced the customary evasions. Nevertheless, the anthropologist estimated that 50% of the total Gypsy population in the state of Washington refused to cooperate with the survey or could not be located. And even when an interview was granted, there was considerable discomfort with many of the questions. The research describes the interview situation as follows:

"During the interview the respondent ordinarily betrayed his unease in many ways; at times he would fail to answer. The questions made little sense to the respondents, despite the precautions of the preparatory phase. This was not so much due to the manner in which the questions were worded as it was to apprehensions about who had sent them or who was going to read the answers. Lack of familiarity with research projects of any kind compounded the problem for researcher and respondent. 'Why,' they would ask, 'do you have to ask everybody these questions when our answers are all the same?' or 'He's my cousin. Just put him down the same as me.' . . . The impersonality of hiring someone to ask questions which they frequently found embarrassing and personal for no better purpose than to learn 'how many' were on welfare, or . . . sent their children to school puzzled them and was frequently taken as an affront to their intelligence. The flippancy of some of the answers undoubtedly affected some of the findings."[26]

Given these limitations, the findings may briefly be summarized as follows: Out of a sample population of 82 households or 421 individuals, located in Seattle, Tacoma, Spokane and other areas, 100% of the adult males were car salesmen, 39% of the females brought in family income through fortune telling; 77% of the adult males and 89% of the adult females had 4 years of formal schooling or less (20% of the males and 50% of the females had none whatsoever) and welfare, first obtained in the thirties, has become "inseparable from the Gypsies' current lifestyle."[27] In fact, the researcher questions her own findings, indicating that 44% of the respondents are receiving public assistance and says, "Personal experience with various Gypsy families over a period of the last eight years suggests that the majority are on welfare most of the time."[28] This is borne out by the statements of several Washington Gypsy leaders.

These findings indicate that the Gypsies are the most poorly educated of all Washington State's—indeed the United States' minorities. An overwhelming majority of them are functional illiterates. No one has heard of a Gypsy anywhere in the U.S. who has completed high school and remained within the culture. This is clearly the greatest

22

hurdle to education, the source of the Gypsies' strong resistance to it. Education is seen as a conduit to the *gajo* world, a threat to culture and community. When I spoke to the Rom—even the *baros*—about Gypsies in Europe with a university education, they were incredulous and their invariable question was, "But is he a *real* Gypsy?"

Miller Stevens, the 60-year-old Tacoma leader, also asked this question, though he has been in the forefront of the move towards Gypsy education. But he sees it basically as the acquisition of "survival skills", "beating the *gajo* at their own game", and he has expressed misgivings about the future of Gypsy culture. He and his brother Ephraim, in Seattle, and members of the Marks family, in Spokane, feel that the Rom have no choice but to at least partially emerge from their long centuries of isolation. Miller Stevens puts it succinctly: "You can't eat your culture".

The birthrate for Gypsies here, as elsewhere in the world, remains high (the average Rom marries at about the age of 15 and does not practice birth control) while the resources are shrinking. Their only escape route leads through—if not to—the *gajo* world. A young Spokane Gypsy spokesman put it this way: "We have to learn your ways to keep ours."

The Culture of the Washington Rom

Despite their near invisibility as a minority group—perhaps because of it—the Washington Roma are culturally conservative and highly resistant to assimilation. Arranged marriages at an early age continue as the norm, and the *kris romani*, or court of elders, is a vital institution. Standards of purity and pollution are meticulously observed; *Romanes* is spoken at home by the youngest as well as the older generation. The six-year-old son of the Spokane leader, a man who has extensive contacts among the politicians and media personalities of the *gajo* world, was asked what he would like to do after completing his education. Would he like to be a lawyer or doctor or political leader? "I want to sell cars and make money", the boy replied readily. The limit of his 5th grade sister's ambition was to join a newly started sewing class for Gypsy women. Yet the oldest boy spoke about possibly becoming a lawyer (he is now in Junior High School) and a leader of his people. The law seems to be a frequently cited profession among those with educational ambitions for themselves or their children. It is a profession which carries no taint or pollution (like medicine), it allows scope for traditionally valued qualities of verbal aggressiveness and shrewdness in transaction with *gajé*, and it offers the community the hope of a really reliable advocate—one of their own—in their entanglements with the system.

As we have seen, purity-pollution concepts are pervasive in Rom culture. This is probably true to a greater degree in the U.S. than in Europe, and in the Northwest than in many other parts of the country. When I told Miller Stevens and his family that I have a Gypsy acquaintance in Europe who is a doctor, they were incredulous, "He couldn't be a real Gypsy," they said, "no real Gypsy would become a doctor."

Most of Washington's Rom are sedentary or semi-sedentary. They live in store-fronts or in houses near highways or shopping centers. The demographic survey referred to above shows that out of 82 households in the sample, 22 of the respondents owned their homes or were in the process of buying them while 58 adults were renting homes.

Yet these figures may be a misleading indication of stability, because a good portion of the population moves about for a part of the year. The reasons for traveling may vary from "looking for work" to "attending weddings, funerals or feasts" or simply visiting relatives. Some Gypsies will emphasize the benefits of travel for its own sake. Traditionally, it was associated with health, luck and the old nomadic ways. Other Rom point out that continual travel was a life-style forced on their society by *Gajo* harassment. Miller Stevens traveled about with his family in his youth but speaks of it without nostalgia. "Here today and gone tomorrow. Who wouldn't rather live in a house like this?" he asks, indicating, with a sweep of his hand, the spacious living room with its red carpets, imitation baroque furniture and color television.

The survey nevertheless indicated that 10 of the informants had moved once with their entire household within the past year, while 21 had moved more than once in that time, one as many as ten times. The researcher notes that even these figures are biased in the direction of stability because, shortly after the survey was made, a number of the Oregon Gypsies who were then "temporarily" in Washington due to the troubles in Portland, sold their homes. (I have since been told that most of them have returned.)

There is still a strong tendency towards the traditional Gypsy response to trouble of all kinds: pack up and leave. In the past, it prevented the accumulation of property other than the most portable. Traditionally much of the surplus wealth—when there was any—would be invested in gold and silver jewelry worn by the women. As the Gypsies began to move to the cities, they also began to acquire more property: furniture, clothing, electrical appliances. Yet, when there is trouble, the values of the nomadic life prevail. If there is nonportable property, sell it, leave it to a relative, or, if necessary, abandon it. This is not considered "running away" in Rom, as it is in *gajo* culture. It is a socially approved method of problem-solving developed over centuries of existence as a powerless and continually harassed minority group.

In addition to household moves, a large proportion of the informants had reported out-of-town trips ranging in duration from one week to six months for social, ceremonial or economic reasons. James Marks II, of Spokane, estimates that 50% of Washington's Rom are on the move at any one time:

> It varies with the jobs they have . . . when it snows they try to go to California, where the weather's better and they can move a little. When it's cold and icy Gypsies don't have much work . . . they don't work in a grocery store, they don't work in a hardware store, they don't work in a bank . . .

There is still strong social disapproval for working for wages for the *gajo*. The Washington Rom are even more conservative in this respect than are Rom in many other parts of the U.S., not to speak of Europe, where Gypsies are found in a variety of non-traditional occupations, ranging from factory work to medicine.

Miller Stevens and other northwest Rom worked in the Kaiser Shipyards in Portland during World War II. (One of his sons, born during this period, is named "Kaiser".) It was the only time in his life that he worked for the *gajo*. When asked why he did it, he replied:

> "Money . . . it was hard to get money in those days and any way you could get a few dollars in, we did it."

On the other hand, when asked "how was fortune-telling during the war," the unanimous answer that came from the older women present, as well as Miller, was "beautiful" and "much better than now", so it can be assumed that there was additional income from that source. Presently, the majority of fortune tellers complain of depressed business. One reason may be found in competition from a proliferation of counselors and therapists of various kinds such as psychologists, social workers, gurus, etc.

Fortune telling is an ancient art, passed on from mother to daughter and, as has been noted, reserved exclusively for the *gajo*. The *ofisia*, or fortune-telling establishment, is often chosen and publicized by the men. It may be the store front in which the whole family lives, or a separate establishment. The sign in front usually proclaims that inside is a "spiritual advisor" or some such counselor, in order to avoid clashing

with laws against fortune telling which exist in many states and municipalities.

The technique in this area is inevitably palmistry, although in some other parts of North America and in Europe, cards, and even phrenology have been used. Ronald Lee's wife, a Canadian Indian, learned to tell fortunes with his mother's pack of tarot cards after their marriage.

Women can achieve high status in Rom society through their success at fortune-telling. It is generally recognized that such success stems more from psychological skills, such as shrewdly sizing up the needs of a client and speaking to them, than from any innate talent for communing with the supernatural. Thus a potential daughter-in-law *(bori)* who is known as a successful fortune-teller is a great asset to her husband's family and will command a commensurately high brideprice.

In the survey, 50% of the adult male respondents had never worked at a *gajo* job, and of those who had, the majority worked as children shining shoes or as teenagers washing or parking cars, as gas station attendants, etc. This kind of employment almost invariably terminated with marriage, at which time, regardless of age, the Gypsy boy becomes a Rom or man. Of those who had held adult *gajo* jobs, the majority fell into the older age brackets and mostly, like Miller Stevens, had worked in some defense plant during World War II. Only 3 of the younger men reported working for wages and all of them came from the eastern U.S. One of these said he had moved to the Northwest in order to get into the car business.

The foregoing strongly suggests a non-diversified and culturally conservative orientation to occupation on the part of the Northwestern Rom, in comparison to other parts of the country or to other periods in history.

This conservatism is expressed in many spheres of Rom life, and always functions to draw the line between *Rom* and *gajo*—to maintain a social and cultural isolation while interacting with the dominant society in a number of prescribed ways. These have been developed into a fine art through centuries of practice. The need to draw boundaries together with the strong cultural sanctions for maintaining them—such as the penalty of *marimé*—have permitted the Rom to survive with their culture intact. In addition, the strong family system and the continued relatively high mobility have kept them from following the usual American immigration patterns. It has allowed them to resist both assimilation of the second generation and the culture of poverty, despite their lack of literacy and vocational skills.

Whether this situation will continue as increasing exposure to the *gajo* world erodes the Gypsies' cultural defenses is questionable. Ronald Lee makes a grim prognosis for the Canadian Rom, whose situation in many ways resembles that of their bretheren in the U.S.:

> As long as the authority of the *Kris* or the patriarchal judges holds them in check and the *Romania* is enforced, everything will be all right, since these judges are old men who remember the past . . . but once they are gone (and they are going fast) they will be replaced by leaders born in the slums . . . when this does come about the police will not be dealing with illegal fortune-tellers, illegal salesmen, illegal used car dealers or illegal stove mechanics (i.e. working without a license) but they may possibly find themselves dealing with a set of gangsters, hold-up artists, thugs and criminals speaking their own secret language, having a strong organization, and full of nothing but hatred for and contempt of the society around them. This we are trying to prevent, and there is still time, but the sands are running out fast.[29]

It remains to be seen whether the new consciousness stirring among them can head off such a future. The strong fear of the teen-age delinquent sub-culture to which schooling might expose their children is evidence of their misgivings. The hostility expressed toward the author of "King of the Gypsies" for exposing the criminal activities of the Bimbo clan in New York reflects the Rom's distaste for being identified with illegal activities.

Already for many Gypsies welfare has become a way of life. How long can they resist other aspects of the culture of poverty? The leaders are coming to realize that new forms of dealing with these threats from *gajo* society must be found; withdrawal is no longer possible.

The strong antipathy to education and intermarriage has prevented the formation of "intermediate groups" among the Rom, from which the leadership for advancement and change is drawn in other minority groups. In Europe new Romani movements have been created and led by a small but growing Rom intelligentsia, many of whose members are products of mixed marriages. But in America this has not happened, least of all in the Northwest. It is remarkable, therefore, that it is precisely from this area that the strongest movement toward ethnic awareness, education and change should have come. It is the leadership of the Washington Roma, themselves illiterate and traditional, that has placed the Gypsies on the ethnic map of the U.S. We will now examine how this came about.

28

Leadership, Education and Change in Washington Rom Society

The changes which are now beginning to stir within Washington State's Rom community can be traced to the activities of a very few individuals. Foremost among these is Miller Stevens, a used car dealer for the *gajo* world, but a respected *baro* for the Rom. During the late 1960s, he watched the growing militancy of ethnic minority groups throughout the state of Washington and elsewhere. He saw the gains that Black, Chicano, Indians and others were making in American society through organization, education and assertiveness, and he wondered if the Rom could not do the same.

In 1968, he traveled to Washington, D.C., to meet with Department of Health, Education and Welfare officials about the plight of his people, many of whom were subsisting on welfare and most of whom were illiterate. He succeeded in having the Gypsies declared an official ethnic minority by HEW, which made them eligible for a variety of new programs. His first project was the establishment of a Head Start program for Gypsy children, conducted out of his store-front home during the summer of 1968. It began with about 15 children, many of them his own grandchildren, and was funded by a small grant from the Office of Economic Opportunity.

The next step was to reach some of the adults, the overwhelming majority of whom were, like Miller Stevens, illiterate. While few of them were prepared to return to school with their children, a project sponsored by the Division of Vocational Rehabilitation soon caught on. As was mentioned previously, virtually all adult Gypsy males in Washington are involved in buying and selling cars. Under Miller's prodding, the DVR set up a program combining basic literacy and accounting skills with on-the-job training in Stevens' car lot. In the past, the written test which was required for obtaining a license prevented them from practicing their trade legally for the most part. This program related directly to their needs, and soon six adult Gypsy men were enrolled for the two years of adult education and one year on-the-job training. As part of the informal deal, Stevens arranged that these six men would also obligate themselves to send their children to school.

The DVR counselor who worked with the Gypsies described some of the problems they encountered:

> "The first Gypsy men applying for service would only apply as a group . . . they were accepted as a group, and out of fear would only see a doctor or a psychologist as a group."[30]

Their fear was so great that at first the adult education classes had to be held in Gypsy homes. "But as fear and apprehension disappeared, they moved into the same school the children attend." [31]

Despite the initial apprehension, the program was, for the small number involved, very successful. Five out of the six received loans from the Small Business Administration and set up their own used car lots in Western Washington. Since its inception in 1969, the program has trained 18 men (as of April, 1976). The energy crisis has created more problems for them, as Gypsies generally stock only large American cars. Consequently, according to the DVR counselor, some have left their lots to return to older, more informal methods of dealing, but now with licenses.

In Seattle, Miller Stevens' brother, Ephraim, was working on other programs for the Rom. In the early 1970s, he worked as a community organizer for the Seattle-King County Economic Opportunity Board. His big project was to push for a Gypsy multi-service center, modeled on one proposed by the Chicano leadership in Seattle. The project became embroiled in controversy when it reached the City Council. For a short time in the spring of 1973, Seattle newspapers were carrying almost daily articles, editorials and letters to the editor about an ethnic group that most residents of Washington did not know existed. The lead of one article in the Seattle Post-Intelligencer of March 7, 1973, provides the flavor:

"Three city councilmen fiddled with a Gypsy request for an ethnic center yesterday but failed to agree on the need for such a facility."

Ephraim Stevens' request had come at a strategic moment. Shortly before, five members of the council had voted to give some $131,000 to a Chicano Center after the Chicanos occupied an old school. The Gypsies were demanding equal time and money from the city. The councilman who opposed the center on the grounds that the Gypsy population was too small—about 150 all year around and about 500 in the summer, was placed on the defensive by the accusation that one ethnic group was being favored over another, and promptly took some action on the Gypsies' long-standing complaints that the written examinations for used car lot licenses and the city ordinance banning fortune telling had taken away their livelihood. He enlisted the aid of the city Ombudsman to assist the Gypsies in taking oral exams for licenses and requested the council to immediately repeal the anti-fortune telling ordinance.

A Gypsy Community Center was set up in Seattle and Ephraim Stevens became its "Gypsy counselor". A separate school was set up for children. It started with 6, and soon increased to 25. There was also an evening literacy class at the Center. The teacher was a university student whom Ephraim and some friends met at a restaurant and casually hired.

Today only the school is still functioning and Ephraim is no longer associated with it, a matter about which he freely expresses his resentment.

> "I hired a teacher and she took over the program and now the American people is runnin' it . . . I put it together, I done everything, I worked 2 years for it . . . but there's no Gypsy associated with it any more . . . it's right where I left it. You see, they took me out of it because I was demanding a lot of stuff from them, they thought I was pushing it . . . I built it up from the ground . . . I built it from 6 kids to 25 kids, I even told them how to bring the Gypsy kids in there . . . and just after it was going real good, they figured because I can't read or write, I don't have a place at the school . . ."

Ephraim remembers his job for the Model Cities Program with some bitterness: "They gave me a job for 2 months to keep me quiet; then they just let me come in and use the office." There was also a DVR program in Seattle like the one in Tacoma, training men to become legitimate used car dealers. But it is no longer functioning. I asked why and he said,

"It's the DVR, it hasn't got any more programs." When asked whether they had run out of money, he replied, "I don't know, they usually give you that when they don't want to sponsor your program."

The activist in Spokane is James Marks II, who calls himself "Senator of the Gypsy nation." He is young (29), energetic and, despite his illiteracy, seems to relate easily to the *gajo* world. His home, furnished in the more or less standard Gypsy style—red carpeted, damask-draped opulence—contained framed letters and photographs on the wall, indicating "the Senator's" familiarity with the political, religious and media luminaries of the day. His correspondents include President Ford, Senators Jackson and Magnuson, and Governor Evans. He seems to have a hot line to the press and television and made himself known as spokesman for the Gypsies of the Northwest, if not of America. (Other Rom, with whom I spoke, clearly do not share this feeling. Asked why he calls himself "Senator" he replied that "Gypsy Kings" were too commonplace. "Senator" would make people take notice.)

Yet Marks seems to have many of the same goals as Miller and Ephraim Stevens. The foremost among these is education, and he speaks of this with a passionate conviction:

"I want my children and other Gypsy children to have the opportunity to have reading and writing so they could go and lonk for a job and then if they don't give it to them they could not say they're Gypsies, or they're ignorant or they're just unqualified. I have went to many *gaje* and asked for jobs and a lot of them say you don't have reading skills, you don't have writing skills, you don't have vocational skills, you don't have no kind of training . . . and what can I say, I don't . . . Education is the key to success; all other minorities is benefitted, we must, we must learn to read and write. It's the only way . . ."

Marks, a natural orator, can quickly exchange the weapons of persuasion for those of coercive legal action. His lack of formal education does not prevent him from having a good grasp of power relationships and a surprisingly sophisticated understanding of the intricacies of government bureaucracy. In March, 1975, Marks' great-uncle, Steve Marks, described in an Associated Press dispatch as "king of America's estimated 250,000 Gypsies", died in Kansas. His body was shipped to Portland for burial in the Rose City Cemetery, one of the largest Gypsy burial grounds in the U.S. Marks had made a deposit with a local funeral home, but when the owner discovered him to be a Gypsy, he refused the body. Thereupon, Marks filed a complaint with the civil rights division of the Oregon Bureau of Labor. This unprecedented action caused a number of traditional-minded Gypsies to boycott the funeral and the wake.[32]

The programs in Spokane are similar to those in Seattle and Tacoma: a school where a few children attend sporadically, some adult education, and now a sewing class for Gypsy women, a program co-sponsored by the city and by the Work Exchange for Young Adults. The children attend night classes twice a week in a Headstart program supported by the City of Spokane. So far, there is no day school for Gypsy children. The adults accompany their children to the converted World War II barracks and many learn to read with them. The three school-age children of Marks are attending both the *gajo* day school and the Gypsy night school.

In addition, Marks set up a Gypsy Cultural Center, with some outside help. It lasted for about six months and then was discontinued for lack of funds. Marks claims he went to various foundations without success. Like Ephraim Stevens and Miller Stevens, he is bitter about it:

"This Gypsy cultural center was the only one in existence in the U.S. The directors and the curators and most important, the consultants and the artists were all Gypsies. We tried very much to establish this Center in Spokane . . . but nobody seemed to really support it. We tried the Washington State Art Commission not once, not twice, but many times

33

to get a grant, with no response . . . there wasn't one penny that came to the Gypsy Cultural Center . . . we tried with the Washington State Bicentennial Commission on a project . . . and they didn't even try to help us . . . I went to many foundations, I went to Ford Motors, General Motors, I went to local level, state level, I don't understand that, for something we have and nobody really took the time out and see what we have . . ."

One can sense a profound feeling of alienation in the words of these men who are trying to lead their people toward emerging from their centuries of isolation and coming to terms with 20th century America. They all mentioned the advantages enjoyed by other, more militant minorities. And they all alluded, with special bitterness, to the money spent on settling the Vietnamese refuges, who are "not even American citizens". Marks puts it this way:

"We had a number of good ideas but there was no money to support it . . . With all the money that goes to minorities and . . . culture and educational programs, why wasn't there a few people to help us. They seemed to help the Blacks, many many times, they gave so much money to the Indians God himself couldn't help them any more, why couldn't they give us a few dollars? We wasn't asking for the world . . . look at the thousands they gave the Vietnamese, they ain't even American citizens, Vietnamese killed their sons . . .

Yet despite the complaints regarding the meagerness of funds, all the Gypsy leaders emphasize that Washington State's programs are groundbreaking and being watched carefully by Gypsies in other parts of the nation. Ephraim Stevens is helping to start a program in Chicago. Miller Stevens has received a grant from H.E.W. to bring the news of his programs to Gypsies in 5 different states. James Marks II spends a considerable amount of time traveling about the country and speaking at Gypsy functions. They all say there is a considerable amount of interest in the programs. Marks describes the reception he got in his travels about the country last summer:

"There's very much interest . . . Gypsies come from 5, 6, 700 miles just to hear me speak about these educational programs and these vocational programs and the subject, the question is the same thing, how could they start it, how can we take part, who can we go to, we want to do it for our children."

Marks' activities have expanded from local to national and international levels. He recently became curator of the small Gypsy collection—put together by Marks—of the Smithsonian Institution. Marks brought to the attention of officials of the Smithsonian that although most other minority groups were represented in the Bicentennial displays, the Gypsies were not. So after a "trial run" of exhibiting at

Joey Stevens and Joey George from Gypsy Alternative School, Seattle.

35

the Spokane Expo in 1974, he turned his attention to Washington, D.C. He collected artifacts from different Gypsy communities and put together an exhibit for the Smithsonian. The most important piece, he says, is the *stargo*, the "official Gypsy flag", a red chiffon scarf, about 2 yards long fastened to an axe handle. There are three ribbons attached to the scarf, each representing a *vitsa*. On the ribbons are fastened 6 coins of 6 European countries, representing a dowry for the bride. This banner was apparently used for marriages. Associated with it is a brass wedding bell, which summoned the ancestors to join the ceremony.

Another exhibit Marks described was a tapestry presumably used on a covered wagon which came West from Wichita, Kansas, during the days of the Gold Rush in 1849. There were represented on it two branches of the Gypsies' fortune telling craft, palmistry and phrenology. The pioneers, according to Marks, had need of more than food and protection in their trek across the plains. And the Gypsy "49ers" filled this need. The historical accuracy of this story has not so far been substantiated.

While Marks has a strong sense of tradition, like most other Rom, he has very little knowledge of history. While he first suggested that the Gypsies came west en masse at the time of the Gold Rush, he said later:

> "I don't really know when they came, they came when all the immigrants came."

Miller Stevens was also vague about the Gypsies' migration West and in response to my question, said he had "read" in the newspapers that they came in covered wagons in 1901. Few Washington Gypsies can trace their own family backgrounds back more than about four generations. Despite their carefully preserved traditions, they are a people without a history. The new leaders realize the drawbacks of this and lament the fact that what knowledge they have of their past comes from the *gajo*. When speaking about the Gypsies' Indian origins, Ephraim Stevens made the following proposal:

> "Don't you think that you might get one Gypsy to travel in Europe and have sponsored by the government and really find out about the Gypsies where they belong. Because all we have is your word and somebody else's that we came from India, like somebody says we come from Rumania, you know there's a lot of people that said that . . . we've never been to Rumania . . . anybody can say that . . . I think it would be a very smart idea for you . . . to say 'actually what we need is a couple of Gypsies to go around with us and find definitely where the

Gypsies come from' . . . you say we come from India, I say to my wife 'we come from India', (she says) 'no, no I'm not Indian'. Well, who said, just because they said we're supposed to be from India? Now if we get one of our groups to go over there and to find out and to take films and do a lot of things, just exactly what you're doing, but with a Gypsy, the Gypsies will recognize more than what they do if you were saying it . . . all the Gypsies they think they're actually from Serbia, my old man used to tell me, they all came from Serbia, from Serbia, they split up . . ."

Ephraim Stevens' wife, a Greek Gypsy from Chicago, disputed the idea of Serbian origins because she knew her father was born in Athens. Interestingly enough, the language of the country of the immigrant Rom's birth seems to become lost to the second generation, following the pattern of other immigrant groups in America. This is not, of course, the case with the Rom's own language, *Romanes*. Once again, we see the mechanisms of Rom isolation and self-preservation at work: the *gajo* name, language, nationality, even religion, are easily exchanged —they are, after all, only covers to preserve their real identity.

Formal nationality, particularly, has always been a matter of little importance to the Gypsies, despite periodic declarations of allegiance to one nation or another. It is one reason that it makes being a refugee easier for Gypsies than for most other people. Jan Yoors, a Belgian artist now living in the U.S., traveled with a *kumpania* of Lowara Rom before World War II. During the war, as a member of the Resistance, he succeeded in organizing many of them to smuggle goods and personnel for the Allies. He wrote about the terrible fate of the Gypsies who were deported to Nazi concentration camps, but he noted that of those who survived to join the hordes of displaced persons who were roaming Europe after the conclusion of the war, the Gypsies fared much better than most. Accustomed throughout their existence to being stateless and on the move, they did not suffer the *anomie*, the personal and social disorganization that have become the marks of refugees. Even as the Germans advanced in the latter stages of the war, Yoors described the Rom joining the fleeing civilian populations "with a clearer sense of purpose, with greater dignity" than the others.[33]

On a smaller scale, the transatlantic immigration of European Gypsies continues, often via Canada or Mexico, and usually with some degree of confusion regarding their passports and national status. The latest such incident took place in Quebec, where 22 members of the Petrov clan had been detained by Canadian immigration authorities for illegally entering Canada on stolen Italian passports which they had purchased for $75 apiece. Led by their 70-year-old *baro*, Nikola

Petrov, the group had wandered through Russia, Bulgaria and Yugoslavia before embarking for Canada. A few years earlier a group of 45 Yugoslav Rom had appeared in Montreal with illicit West German passports. They were ordered deported but, while the order was being appealed, they vanished—presumably across the U.S. border, which they had tried to cross earlier, to join relatives.[34]

A small number of this continuing stream of immigration reaches the Northwest. According to Ephraim Stevens, many came just before and during World War II. But the Rom already in the area carefully control the territory and permission must be obtained from the local *kumpania* before the newcomers can settle.

"At present, the territorial aspects of social organization are of focal concern", the recent demographic survey of Washington's Roma concluded.[35] Newcomers are increasingly seen as a threat. As traditional occupations became obsolete, few new specialties came to replace them, and with a rapidly multiplying Rom population, the competition is growing keen. It is rumored that some Gypsy spokesmen, while publicly condemning city and state ordinances against fortune-telling, privately encourage them in order to maintain their own monopoly, informally arranged with the *gajo* authorities. One Gypsy was said by another to control access to the welfare system in a particular city. The effect of all this is a considerable degree of tension and factionalism, sometimes resulting in open conflict. Sometimes a *kris* will have to be convened to deal with the problems of territoriality.

From this situation comes one of the strongest internal pressures towards change. Far-sighted *baros* such as Miller Stevens see that internal conflict can only lead to self-destruction. He sees education as the only way out of the trap. In terms of the requirements of modern society, it would seem still a limited vision, confined to the males and not going much beyond a junior high school level.

The Gypsy fear of contamination in every sense, the strong desire to maintain the integrity of language and culture, is always in a precarious balance with the felt need for survival skills in 20th century, urban America. One who promotes literacy in Rom society is regarded as a radical. Both 60-year-old Miller Stevens and 29-year-old James Marks II have been tarred by this brush and experienced considerable opposition from conservative members of the community. Marks sees the conflict primarily in generational terms, Stevens more in terms of ideology. Both have expressed themselves strongly against assimilation and intermarriage.

Rom and Gajo in a Period of Transition

During the past few years, the Roma of Washington State have been reaching out in many directions. Through the awareness that led to their demand for minority status and its benefits, they have been groping in other directions, too. They have made contacts with international as well as national organizations. Several leaders have been contacted by the International Committee of Roma, which has its headquarters in Paris. The U.S. delegate of this organization is Ian Hancock, a professor at the University of Texas, a rare—probably unique—occupation for a North American Rom. Miller Stevens has also spoken on the telephone with Ronald Lee, the Canadian delegate to the I.C.R. Marks has recently been designated as a regional representative by Vanko Rouda, a French lawyer who is President of the organization.

The Washington Roma have also been brought into contact with representatives of another Paris-based organization, an evangelical group that has made considerable inroads among French Roma. The connecting link here is a state government official who supervised the DVR program in Tacoma and became deeply involved with his Gypsy clients.

Whether the new contacts being made are with foreign, educated Roma or *gaje*, the Washington Roma making them are forced into a new kind of interaction with *gajo* individuals and institutions. Traditional Rom-Gajo relationships followed a fairly clear pattern. They were symbolic or mutually exploitive, depending on the perspective of the observer. But they were almost always confined to the economic sphere, and on a one-to-one basis, such as the fortune teller and her client. The Gypsies' fleeting encounters with *Gajo* institutions came when they ran afoul the law and found themselves in jail, when they were, from time to time, caught in the net of the military or educational establishments, or when they began to develop regular relations with the Welfare bureaucracy.

But now, for the first time, *baros* like Miller Stevens began to deal with *gajo* institutions not as individuals temporarily trapped by force of economic need, but as representatives of Roma as an ethnic group. In the course of his work on behalf of the various projects initiated by him, he met with bureaucrats of all levels and attended meetings with other minority leaders. He listened to the demands of blacks, Chicanos, Native Americans and others; he observed their strategies, their successes and failures. He learned what resources were available to his people under their new designation as "minority". He came to realize,

39

more than ever, the degree to which education provided the key to survival. He saw that other minority leaders were asserting their peoples' needs and rediscovering their traditions, not in spite of education, but through it. It was the educated Indians, blacks and Chicanos who were able to explore their groups' history and preserve their traditions.

As a result of these and other experiences, Miller Stevens undertook projects that would have been unheard of a few years earlier, particularly for a Gypsy of his age and background. He not only became actively involved in educational programs, but he collaborated with a *gajo* anthropologist on a Gypsy census, with a *gajo* linguist on a project to collect folktales and devise an orthography for *Romanes* so that, one day, Gypsy children could read and write it themselves. All of this involves revealing rather than concealing, which had been the traditional mode of interaction with the *gajo*.

James Marks' various exhibits and short-lived Gypsy Cultural Center reflected this change as well. While Gypsies were long a familiar sight at fairs and carnivals, now they were exhibiting their culture rather than selling their wares in Spokane at the Expo, and at the Bicentennial Folklife Festival in Washington, D.C. For the first time in the U.S., they were putting themselves on exhibit as an ethnic group. It was a radical departure. Also, for the first time, *Gaje* had to be related to as something other than customers or persecutors. They were not yet friends, but they began to be accepted as teachers, counselors, and learners. Also, they came to be known as dispensers of funds, and soon the Gypsy leaders became adept grantsmen, as they had quickly become shrewd car salesmen when their more traditional occupations became obsolete.

While they are skillful at the wheeling and dealing, the bargaining that is a part of political leadership in the *gajo* world, there is a large residue of suspicion and ambivalence toward revealing elements of Rom culture. "Why should we tell you our secrets?" they say, "nobody is paying us for it." Traditionally, money has been their one link to the *gajo* world; they were accustomed to providing services for which they would be paid. They have not yet learned to translate intangibles such as publicity into their accounting system. They realize—at least some of the leaders do—that they can no longer remain invisible if they are to claim their slice of the American cake. At the same time, the sudden spotlight can be blinding. So, when Peter Maas' book about the criminal activities of the Bimbo clan appeared *(King of the Gypsies*, Bantam Books, 1975), Miller Stevens asked to appear on the Today Show to represent his people, whom, he felt, had been maligned by the book. The trouble is that neither he, nor any of the other leaders, were able to read the book. (Marks claims that he has whole books put on tape.) And when he was asked some questions about Gypsy marriage customs, he replied "no comment".

Thus, the tug between secrecy and revelation is always there in the relations between the Rom and the new kind of *Gaje* with whom they have been interacting, i.e. bureaucrats, social workers, journalists and entertainment audiences. That vague quantity called "public opinion" is something they must suddenly take account of. Thus, they are beginning to monitor stereotypes of Gypsies purveyed by the mass media. The rather scurrilous review of Peter Maas' book in *Newsweek*— which in some ways was more damaging than the book itself—was quickly responded to by a Romani from New York, a high school graduate and secretary. She wrote:

> "Your review of Peter Maas' book "King of the Gypsies" seriously stereotypes and defames the Gypsies. Peter Maas has written about a certain group of people within the Gypsy society who are disliked by the rest of the community, and has made them out to be representative of the manner in which we all live. He has stated that we are illiterate and uneducated people. I happen to be a Gypsy; I am a high school graduate and hold a job as a secretary in a New York City office, and in many European countries, there are Gypsy men and women who hold jobs as lawyers, doctors, secretaries and teachers. Maas has forgotten to write about us—the ones working to change the prejudiced attitudes toward us and to better our lives."[36]

Ian Hancock recently wrote to the American Civil Liberties Union, objecting to a television feature in which he perceived negative stereotypes of Gypsies. When a new Jack Lemmon film appeared in Seattle, called "Alex and the Gypsy", Ephraim Stevens and his wife were watching it a few hours after they were informed of its existence. Ronald Lee has been busy combatting Gypsy stereotypes in the Canadian media for many years.

It is inevitable that, as the Rom emerge from their invisibility, old stereotypes will be revived. "They will accuse us of stealing chickens and babies again," Marks said. And his children spoke of the way they were taunted in school. They called them "dirty Gypsy", "fortune-teller", "thief", very much like the names their great grandparents were called by the *gaje* of their day. Ancient stereotypes, derived from the European countryside, are dusted off and applied to these urban nomads of late 20th century America. These are reinforced by best-selling novels and hit songs about "Gypsy love", campers called "Gypsy rovers" and irregular operations such as "gypsy cabs".

The new encounter between Rom and *Gajo* may be traumatic on both sides. The modern American, equipped with nothing but old stereotypes about a people he thought no longer existed, is suddenly thrown into an encounter with individuals whom he may have mistaken for dark-skinned slum dwellers from one minority group or another. He finds himself facing a thoroughly integrated member of a culture that has barely changed for centuries. There has been a greater continuity in the European's relation to Gypsies; he never really lost sight of them. The colorful caravans continued to roam the countryside of western European countries; government subsidies perpetuated the song and dance and folklore of the Gypsies of communist countries. There is scarcely a restaurant in Budapest without its Gypsy ensemble, to charm both natives and tourists. In other words, Gypsies never went underground.

But in the U.S. and particularly in the state of Washington, they have stepped suddenly from the pages of old romances and albums into the American ethnic mosaic. Peter Maas relates, in the introduction to his book, how this assignment to write about the Gypsies plunged him into a state of culture shock, where he could not fall back on "a common ground of word meanings, of aspirations and attitudes, motivations, hopes and fears".[37] At the same time, he was amazed and intrigued by the sudden discovery of "so many gypsies . . . living essentially as they had for hundreds of years, blithely escaping the massive surveillance and computerization that has been increasingly bugging the rest of us".[38]

While writers and even hard-nosed social scientists who deal with Gypsies have found themselves seduced by this somewhat romanticized life-style, bureaucrats who have suddenly had to deal with them as clients have experienced considerable frustration in trying to comprehend their multiple identities and irregular habits. This has often expressed itself as irritation with even the legitimate requests. In Washington, where more state bureaucracies have come into contact with Gypsies than perhaps any other state, this attitude often becomes evident. I attended a school board meeting with one of the Gypsy leaders, in which an attempt was made to set up a separate school for Gypsy children. The sticking point was that the *baro* insisted that the school be located on his property, whereas the board wanted it on regular school grounds. They thought that they had already gone more than half way to meet his separatist demands by permitting the use of an old building on school property and agreeing to use a Gypsy teacher's aide. They suspected his insistence was somehow linked to his hope of obtaining a tax benefit or other economic gain from the location of the school on his property. The *baro*, on the other hand, thought that their refusal to accede to such a simple and necessary arrangement reflected their determination to sabotage the whole project. He emphasized that Gypsy parents would refuse to send their children to a hostile *gajo* environment, while in familiar surroundings they could be persuaded to come to school. Is not that what they all wanted? He could not understand why these *gaje* repeatedly frustrated the common goals with technical-legal barriers. Roma had always known how to get around such obstacles and they assumed that if *gaje* did not, it meant they were not really interested in the results.

In another Washington city, an official recommended to his superior in Olympia that a proposed project not be initiated because of factional disputes within the Gypsy community. He described a 2½-hour meeting in his office with 15 members of the Gypsy community as "total chaos". He was taken aback by their style of debate and felt that they were less interested in the "rehabilitative" benefits of the particular project than in the opportunity it afforded them for "exploitation of the state of Washington".[39]

On the other hand, a few sensitive government officials have understood that the Gypsies' situation is different from that of other minorities and have, within the limits of the law, attempted to accede to their strong desire for separate facilities. They realize that it is not only a question of ideology but of centuries of fear and rigid cultural rules of purity and pollution, which reinforce their separateness in sacred as well as secular terms. Such an official in Tacoma wrote in a report:

> "It has been evident from the very beginning that the traditional methods of training would have to be abandoned. Their fear of the non-Gypsy 'establishment' vocational and public schools is too great to overcome overnight. The mores of the average Gypsy, particularly the older generation, will not allow them to use a public restroom, and they refrain from public eating facilities or from eating food prepared by non-Gypsies."[40]

In these first steps towards even a limited integration into American society, the *Rom* fear not only ritual pollution. In arguing for separate schools, for a separate cultural center in Seattle, the same reasons are advanced: the *Rom* are a distinct people, with their own language and cultural identity, with a social structure that has thus far resisted the onslaughts of alienation and rootlessness that are the curse of western civilization. The *Rom* fear the pollution of drugs and promiscuity, with

Gypsy Child.

its dreaded correlate, venereal disease, a condition that renders the individual *marimé*. In his request to the city council for a separate Gypsy center, Ephraim Stevens said:

> "My sons are old-fashioned boys. I don't want them corrupted by other teen-agers . . . the things that go on . . . cigarettes, dope . . . you'll never find these things in a Gypsy center."[41]

These feelings, shared by almost all adult Gypsies, regardless of their attitudes towards education and social programs, create a dilemma for government agencies trying to assist them. How can demands for separatism be reconciled with the ideal of integration? To some extent, this dilemma extends to minority group policies in general, but relations with the *Rom* represent it in its clearest form. The new minority militancy and resulting policies of socio-cultural pluralism, oblige the government to take note of and extend its services to any ethnic minority that declares itself as such. At the same time, there is considerable resistance to extreme demands of separatism on both ideological and legal grounds. These conflicting attitudes emerged in the debate over the demand for a Gypsy Center in Seattle.

In February of 1973, Ephraim Stevens presented his request for a Gypsy multi-service center to the City Council's Parks and Public Grounds Committee, soon after the Council had voted the funds for a Chicano center. The Chairman of the Committee and the President of the City Council, himself a member of an ethnic minority, were skeptical about separate centers for all of Seattle's minorities. Extravagant references to Zanzibarian centers in Seattle's future were made by the Chairman. A Councilman who had opposed the funding of the Chicano Center stated his belief that various ethnic groups should share the cultural centers set up by the Model Cities Program. He added: "That is the whole idea, integration, not separation." [42]

A Councilwoman, who had also voted against the separate Chicano Center, asked how the city could provide such a Center for one ethnic group and refuse it to another. She also opposed separate ethnic Centers in principal, although her pleas for even-handedness on the part of the Council made the Gypsies perceive her as an ally. Ephraim Stevens took a similar line of approach in repeating his request to the Committee:

> "Saying no to one group while giving to another is unconstitutional, incriminating and prejudicial."[43]

Nevertheless, the committee unanimously rejected Stevens' proposal.

The fundamental dilemma of the Council was echoed in an unnecessarily offensive Seattle *Times* editorial, which described the Gypsy Center proposal as "One of the sillier pieces of business before the City Council these days," and headlined the whole affair as "Ethnic 'chickens' home to roost."[44] The editorial asked:

> "And how does a city policy that encourages ethnic separatism on the one hand square with the ideal and laws on the other aimed at fostering a free, equal and integrated community?"

For the Washington Gypsies, however, integration cannot even be a theoretical goal. As every outsider who has worked with them has observed, they have a strong sense of cultural identity and a determination to resist any programs aimed at, or even having the effect of, undermining their ties to the community. When children approach puberty, they are generally taken out of school and married before American teen-age culture can subvert them. A Spokane *Rom* took his four children out of school when the oldest boy began to go around with a *gajo* crowd. He was afraid that he would get involved with drugs and girls, the father explained.[45]

The Seattle Gypsy School has been held up by some as an example of what can be accomplished with Gypsy children when they are surrounded by their own culture. The Director of Special Projects of the Seattle School Board was enthusiastic. He said it had greatly improved the Gypsy childrens' school attendance record, which used to be the worst in the city. There are now 25-30 children of assorted ages going daily to a barrack-like wooden building on the grounds of the Bagley Elementary School, where they learn the basic educational skills.

The head teacher is a dark young woman from New York, of Italian descent. "They gave me the job because I look like a Gypsy," she maintains. Her assistant, a blonde young woman who could never "pass" had problems of acceptance at first but now seems to be relating well to the children. Both are advocates of separate educational facilities for Gypsies. "They have a sense of themselves like no minority group I ever worked with," the blonde one said. "Without something like this, they would never go to school," the other agreed.

Both feel that one of the large gaps is in the lack of Gypsy educational materials. Miller Stevens in Tacoma is attempting to remedy this situation by cooperating with two University of Washington linguists, specialists in collecting folk tales and creating a written language out of a spoken one. There are a number of projects of this kind under way in Europe, some under the sponsorship of the I.R.C.

Most teachers and social workers who have been working with the *Rom* through the new programs in Washington State have come to understand and sympathize with their need to remain together while they get their feet wet, rather than to be plunged individually and traumatically into the alien American waters. For, despite their nominal citizenship in the U.S.—which they regard as merely an accident of birth—they are indeed aliens, more than any other minority group. "American" is not part of their cultural identity—except, perhaps vis-à-vis Gypsies from other lands. Their superficial adaptation to American life and their agility in disappearing in its crevices can be misleading. They have always been chameleons, taking on the colors of their environment. But it remained camouflage rather than indicating any lasting changes.

An elderly resident of a small Cascade mining town recalled his childhood, when the Gypsies would come with carnivals every summer. He and the other children would go to the fortune-telling tent, just to hear them speak to each of the immigrant miners in their own tongues. "It was amazing," the old-timer said, "they spoke every language without ever going to school."

The immigrants of those days have made way for their children, second generation American ethnics for whom little remains of their European cultural heritage except a name, a dim memory of a language spoken at home by their parents, and a taste for a few exotic dishes on religious holidays. The multi-lingual Gypsies they admired now may address the children of their erstwhile clients only in English rather than in Italian or Spanish or Serbo-Croatian or Ukrainian. But their own language and culture remains as intact as it was in their parents' or grandparents' generations, though they may have changed horses for cars and wagons for mobile homes.

As the *Rom* leaders who are advocating education realize, sadly, this may be the last generation for whom this holds true. Desperately as they want to maintain both the integrity of their culture and acquire for their children the *gajo* tools of survival, they realize the conflicts which are inherent in these two goals. They acknowledge that probably there will be some assimilation, even some intermarriage, whatever they might do to prevent it.

They are standing at the crossroads and asking for help. But in a much deeper sense than the money and the programs, they are *requesting*, today in Washington and tomorrow in many other parts of the country. They are becoming adept in a new form of marketplace haggling with the *gajo*—grantsmanship; so much so, in fact, that some bureaucrats suspect it to be simply a new form of the ancient Gypsy *bujo*, or con game. One Washington State official said, "They want to

47

change their image in everyone's eyes but not their way of doing things." [46]

Yet the Special Projects Director of the Seattle School district, who is responsible for the Gypsy school there, had a more positive attitude towards the traditional Gypsy way of doing things. It was his job to get the children to school. "What did Gypsies dig about *Gajo* culture?" he asked himself. "Simple," he answered himself, "it was money". They refused to go on the bus that was provided for them, he said, "but when we found a way to compensate them for providing their own transportation, it worked like a charm."

This kind of flexible thinking is important when any bureaucracy deals with the Gypsies. It must be understood, for example, that for a Gypsy extracting money from the *Gajo* is not merely an exercise in personal profiteering; it is at once a cultural ritual and the only traditionally approved form of relationship to the outside world. This is why the Gypsies have taken to the welfare system while avoiding other government bureaucracies like the plague. A traditional *Rom* can feel comfortable in relating to the non-Gypsy world in the context of an economic transaction. And it must be remembered that the *baros* of the Northwest who are leading their people in this new direction are still traditional *Rom*.

Yet these *Rom* are asking for more than money, whatever their immediate motives in promoting such projects may be.

They are asking for help at another level and in their unspoken request lies a challenge to American society in this Bicentennial Year. Can this small group of people, who have so long lived as strangers in our midst, be provided with the tools and opportunities for survival in 20th century America without demanding in return an unacceptable price, the price that so many other groups of strangers have had to pay in the past—the extinction of their culture and community? Unlike other immigrants, the Gypsies did not come to America in order to become Americans. Their arrival was simply another lap of a thousand-year westward journey. Only now, after some of them have lived in the United States three or four generations, are they prepared to knock on the door and request entry.

Fortunately for the *Rom* as a distinct community, their knock came at a time when the Melting Pot had at last been put on a back burner. It is no longer the ordeal by fire through which all must pass before they can have access to the American Dream. Instead, there is the Mosaic into which each community can fit without losing its distinctive form or colors.

48

Of course, Melting Pot as well as Mosaic are merely models to which reality only imperfectly conforms. What is important for the Gypsies of Washington and, eventually throughout America, is that the possibility is there. Knowing that education will not automatically signal destruction of all that they value as a people will help to banish the terrors of the unknown road upon which they have taken their first tentative steps.

Ja Devlesa! (Go with God!)

Appendix I

Notes to Text

[1]Werner Cohn, *The Gypsies*, Reading, Mass.: Addison, 1973, p. 23.

[2]Ian Hancock, *Roma: "Gypsies of Texas,"* vol. 1, no.

[3]Anne Sutherland, *Gypsies, the Hidden Americans*, New York: Free Press, 1975.

[4]Ronald Lee, *Goddam Gypsy*, Toronto: Tundra Press, 1973, p. 10.

[5]Ronald Lee, "Gypsies in Canada" *Journal of the Gypsy Lore Society*, vol. XLVI, Jan.-April, 1967, p. 38.

[6]ibid. p. 45.

[7]Jean-Paul Clebert, *The Gypsies*, Harmondsworth: Penguin Books, 1967, p. 16.

[8]Rena C. Gropper, *Gypsies in the City*, Princeton, N.J.: Darwin Press, 1975, p. 17. I am indebted to Gropper for much of the above summary of Gypsy history in the U.S. (pp. 17-21).

[9]Sutherland, op. cit. pp. 240-241

[10]ibid. pp. 32-64.

[11]ibid. p. 202. It is non-Gypsies who "crown" or legitimate "Gypsy kings". The Gypsies often encourage this *gajo* fiction for their own convenience.

[12]Donald Kenrick and Grattan Puxon, *The Destiny of Europe's Gypsies*, N.Y. Basic Books, 1972, p. 23.

[13]ibid., p. 21.

[14]quoted in Vaux de Foletier, *Milles ans de l'histoire tsiganes*, 1970, p. 22. Translated by the author.

[15]ibid.

[16]Bart McDowell, *Gypsies, Wanderers of the World*, N.Y. National Geographic Society, 1970, p. 66.

[17]Kenrick and Puxon, *op. cit.*, p. 157.

[18]ibid., p. 161.

[19]ibid., p. 163.

[20]ibid., p. 164.

[21]op. cit., p. 64.

[22]Lee, 1973, p. 62.

[23]McDowell, op. cit., p. 64.

[24]ibid.

[25]Carol Miller, *"The Roma of Washington State,"* 1973. The demographic information which follows is based on this unpublished paper.

[26]ibid., p. 16.

[27] ibid.

[28] ibid., p. 27.

[29] Lee, 1967, p. 42.

[30] unpublished report to the Division of Vocational Rehabilitation, Robert Frohmader, n.d., p. 3.

[31] ibid., p. 4.

[32] *Seattle Times*, March 11, 1975.

[33] Jan Yoors, *The Gypsies*, 1967, p. 252, see also Yoors, *Crossings*, 1971.

[34] *The Montreal Star*, Aug. 19, 1976.

[35] Miller, op. cit., p. 10.

[36] *Newsweek*, Dec. 1, 1975.

[37] Peter Maas, *King of the Gypsies*, N.Y. Bantam Books, 1975, viii.

[38] ibid.

[39] memo, D.V.R. files.

[40] Frohmader, op. cit., p. 3.

[41] *Seattle Post-Intelligencer*, March 7, 1973.

[42] *Seattle Times*, March 11, 1973.

[43] *Seattle Post-Intelligencer*, March 7, 1973.

[44] *Seattle Times*, March 1, 1973.

[45] *The Wall Street Journal*, April 14, 1976.

[46] ibid.

Appendix II
Selected Bibliography

Clébert, Jean-Paul, *The Gypsies,* Harmondsworth: Penguin Books, 1967.

Cohn, Werner, *The Gypsies,* Reading, Mass: Addison, 1973.

Frohmader, Robert, unpublished report to the Washington State Division of Vocational Rehabilitation, (1971) n.d.

Gropper, Rena C., *Gypsies in the City,* Princeton, N.J.: Darwin Press, 1975.

Hancock, Ian, *Roma, "The Gypsies of Texas,"* vol. 1, no. 1.

Kenrick, Donald and Puxon, Grattan, *The Destiny of Europe's Gypsies,* New York: Basic Books, 1972.

Lee, Ronald, *Goddam Gypsy,* Toronto: Tundra Press, 1973.

—————. *Journal of the Gypsy Lore Society, "Gypsies in Canada",* vol. XLVI, Jan.-April 1967, pp. 38-51.

McDowell, Bart, *Gypsies, Wanderers of the World,* New York: National Geographic Society, 1970.

Maas, Peter, *King of the Gypsies,* New York: Bantam Books, 1975.

Miller, Carol, *"The Roma of Washington State",* Report to the Washington State Department of Social and Health Services, 1973.

—————. *"American Rom and the Ideology of Defilement"* in *Rehfisch,* Farnham, 1975, pp. 41-54.

Rehfisch, Farnham (ed.) Gypsies, *Tinkers and other Travelers,* New York, London, San Francisco; Academic Press, 1975.

Sutherland, Anne, *Gypsies, the Hidden Americans,* New York: Free Press, 1975.

—————. *"The American Rom: A Case of Economic Adaptation"* in *Rehfisch,* 1975, pp. 1-40.

Vaux De Foletier, Francois, *Milles ans d'histoire des tsiganes,* Paris: Fayard, 1970.

Yoors, Jan, *The Gypsies,* New York: Simon & Schuster, 1967.

—————. *Crossings,* New York: Simon & Schuster, 1971.

The Washington State American Revolution Bicentennial Commission
(in cooperation with the Washington State Historical Society and the
Northwest Center for American Folklife and Folklore)

Ethnic History Series

1. Builders, Brewers and Burghers—Germans of Washington State
     by Dale R. Wirsing

2. Straw Hats, Sandals and Steel—The Chinese in Washington State
     by Lorraine Barker Hildebrand

3. The Gypsy in Northwest America
     by Gabrielle Tyrner-Stastny

4. Lairds, Bards and Mariners: The Scot in Northwest America
     by Bruce Le Roy

5. They Walked Before: the Indians of Washington State
     by Cecelia Svinth Carpenter

6. The Italians of Washington State
     by David Nicandri

7. The Yugoslav in Washington State
     by Mary Ann Petrich and Barbara Roje